Original title:
Petals in Prose

Copyright © 2025 Creative Arts Management OÜ
All rights reserved.

Author: Levi Montgomery
ISBN HARDBACK: 978-1-80567-067-4
ISBN PAPERBACK: 978-1-80567-147-3

Fragments of Floral Memory

In the garden, bees take flight,
Chasing dreams on wings of light.
Tulips giggle as they sway,
While daisies whisper jokes all day.

With every bloom, a tale unfolds,
A story ripe, or so I'm told.
Sunflowers wink with cheeky glee,
As petals plot their comedy.

Echoes of Springtime Laughter

Crisp morning air brings jokes galore,
As budding flowers play out their score.
Lavender chuckles in subtle hues,
Daffodils dance in polka-dot shoes.

In this lively, vibrant show,
Even weeds have jokes in tow.
Nature's laughter fills the breeze,
While trees tease the bumblebees.

Sonnet of the Sunlit Garden

In sunlight's glow, the tulips sway,
Taking turns to jest and play.
A rose recites its pick-up line,
While violets giggle, sipping wine.

The lavender sighs, a prankster bold,
Whispers of nectar trickle gold.
Each colorful bloom with giddiness sings,
In this garden of laughter, joy springs.

Rhapsody of Hidden Buds

Beneath the green, a riddle lies,
Where sleepy buds plan their surprise.
A shy petunia, blushing deep,
Dreams of laughter, secrets to keep.

The lilies burst into a cheer,
With every bloom, they persevere.
Underneath the leafy dome,
Floral giggles find their home.

Tales from a Wandering Petal

Upon a breeze, a silly leaf,
Thought it could fly, oh what a belief!
Swirling and twirling, it danced with glee,
Landed on a cat, who startled with a spree.

With laughter loud, the garden stood,
As the leaf discussed its plans for good.
"I'll reach the moon, then have a ball!"
But missed the jump, and down it did fall.

A ladybug, with spots of red,
Said, "You're a dreamer, but you're misled.
Stick to the ground, where you can shine,
Instead of chasing clouds, dear friend divine!"

But off it went, chasing light all day,
Through muddy puddles, in a playful way.
"I'm just a wanderer, can't you see?"
Said the leaf, as it splashed, oh how carefree!

Rhapsody of Flora and Verse

The daisy told a joke to the rose,
But thorns got in the way, I suppose!
Lilies chuckled, not taking it slow,
While daisies blushed, putting on a show.

Sunflowers danced under the sun's glow,
As bees flew around with a humorous flow.
Mixing colors, they painted the air,
Nature's laugh was the sweetest affair.

Whispers of Soft Blooms

Tulips whispered giggles in the breeze,
While the violets played with the honeybees.
A lily lost her cool in the light,
Dancing with shadows until late at night.

Petunias wore hats, quite amusingly grand,
While orchids made jokes that no one could understand.
Bees, clad in stripes, chuckled at the scene,
Giggles and nectar, their daily routine.

Verses of Verdant Dreams

A clover tried rapping, it was quite the sight,
As ferns joined in, oh, what a delight!
Their roots in the rhythm, it felt so alive,
With laughter and leaves, they began to thrive.

Mint plants rolled in, bringing minty fresh cheer,
Telling corny tales that all could hear.
The garden turned wild with a colorful spree,
Underneath the stars, a floral jubilee!

The Language of Blossoms

Dandelions giggled as they floated away,
While roses exchanged puns, come what may.
Jasmine spun tales of a night so bright,
Where vines shared secrets till the morning light.

Lilacs chimed in with a purple-hued jest,
As bumblebees buzzed, they felt quite blessed.
A chorus of blooms, each line a bright cheer,
In the garden of laughter, there's nothing to fear!

Symphony of Soft Touches

In the garden, bees hum bright,
Bouncing here, then taking flight.
The flowers dance in silly guise,
A concert of colors, a sweet surprise.

Butterflies in their fancy dress,
Wiggling on blooms, they never rest.
A sneeze from pollen, oh what a sight,
Nature's giggles, a pure delight!

Petals whisper, secrets they spill,
A wind's gentle push gives them a thrill.
They giggle as the raindrops fall,
A splashy jam session, fun for all.

Each moment catches laughter's breeze,
In this land of flowers, hearts please.
With every flutter, a chuckling cheer,
Nature's own circus, come gather near!

Inkwell of Nature's Fables

Leaves scribble tales on the breeze,
As squirrels play tag among the trees.
A raccoon dons a mask of fun,
Winking at the warm, bright sun.

The brook babbles jokes, oh so spry,
Fish leap out, giving it a try.
Nature writes with vibrant strokes,
With laughter wrapped in playful jokes.

The sun sets in a flamboyant hue,
While owls ask, 'What's on your to-do?'
Writing poems, messy and wild,
Nature's creativity, mischievous child.

Every creature has a part to play,
In this wild tale, come join the fray.
The ink flows freely, laughter awakes,
In this fable land, joy never breaks!

Threads of Delicate Moments

A spider spins her web of dreams,
Catching sunbeams, or so it seems.
Her audience, bugs with wide-eyed stare,
Are tangled in laughter, caught unaware.

Flowers gossip in the glowing light,
Trading zany stories, oh what a sight!
They sway to a rhythm, twist and twirl,
While ants march in a proud little whirl.

Clouds above puff up with pride,
As thunder chuckles, they do not hide.
Lightning strikes a pose — what a show!
Nature's runway, stealing the glow.

Each moment woven with a grin,
In this tapestry, let the fun begin.
Life's little threads, vibrant, absurd,
In every laugh, nature's story is heard!

Garden of Whimsy

In a garden where daisies flirt,
Ladybugs strut, looking dapper in dirt.
They boast of escapades, vivid and bright,
With a giggle, they twirl, what a sight!

The sunflowers cheer, all big and tall,
As they hold a meeting, having a ball.
Gossip flows like nectar in the air,
With laughter and secrets they happily share.

The mushroom's hat is a sight to behold,
With frog friends lounging, so carefree and bold.
They croak the punchline, and all laugh loud,
In this merry garden, joy wraps like a shroud.

Every turn reveals a silly surprise,
Nature's jesters beneath bright skies.
In this realm of whimsy, joy is the key,
A joyful escape, just you and me!

Garden of Fragrant Reflections

In a garden where gnomes take a nap,
The daisies gossip and share a good laugh.
A squirrel steals berries, much to their wrath,
While roses wear sunglasses, all in a flap.

The lilacs are twirling, a dance of delight,
They jest about bees buzzing left and right.
With sunflowers grinning, oh what a sight,
Even broccoli's chuckling, it's quite the night!

Sentences of the Starlit Blossoms

Under the moon, the tulips hold court,
Blabbing of dreams, in a flowery sport.
Petunias are writing a book about farts,
While marigolds giggle, with loose, silly starts.

Daffodils argue on who's got more flair,
As butterflies flutter without a single care.
With rhymes so absurd, no one can compare,
Their wit blooms like daisies, perfume in the air!

The Beneath-Soil Symphony

Down in the dirt, where worms do a jig,
A radish sings loud, 'I'm quite the big pig!'
Carrots are busy in a root vegetable fight,
While turnips tell stories that just aren't quite right.

With a cabbage conductor waving a leaf,
The beetroot admissions are beyond belief.
As onions weep softly, from laughter or grief,
In the symphony below, joy brings relief!

Soliloquy of Swaying Grasses

The grasses are swaying, having a debate,
About which one's fluffiest, oh isn't it great?
The tall blades aspire to reach for the stars,
While clovers just chuckle, beneath buzzing cars.

With whispers of wind and a tickle of dew,
Each blade has a tale, they collectively spew.
In a world where the wind spills secrets so true,
Grass giggles and prances—a green rendezvous!

The Unwritten Words of the Flowers

In the garden where daisies giggle,
Tulips tell tales with a wiggle.
Roses blush red when a bee passes,
Deeds of the day turn into sweet grasses.

Sunflowers wear hats, big and bright,
While violets gossip about the night.
Dandelions dance in the breeze's flow,
Wishes do bloom from their seeds, you know!

Lilies bathe in the morning dew,
Swaying their heads, it's funny but true.
Nature writes verses, oh what a sight,
Words unwritten but shining so bright!

Palette of Scented Memories

A whiff of lavender tickles the nose,
While mint tells jokes and the basil just grows.
Each smell a story, each scent a laugh,
Spilling secrets like a fragrant gaffe.

Cacti with quirks, they're prickly and proud,
Succulents hum songs, drawing quite a crowd.
Aroma adventures in a colorful dance,
Where jasmine's perfume makes everyone prance.

Hibiscus shouts tales of hibiscus tea,
While marigolds snicker with glee.
Memories swirl like confetti in air,
In this fragrant place, there's joy everywhere!

Lyrics from the Budding Meadow

The meadow sings with colors so grand,
Tiny critters choreograph on the land.
Buttercups chuckle, they've seen all the fun,
While grass blades tap dance under the sun.

Bees hum a tune, it's a buzz-tastic song,
And ladybugs waltz as if nothing's wrong.
Every bloom has a story to share,
With laughter resounding if you stop and stare.

Poppies gossip about clouds in the sky,
While larkspur dreams of birds floating by.
Nature's own symphony, cheeky and bright,
In the heart of the meadow, making it right!

Charms of the Whispering Flora

Whispers float softly on the evening breeze,
As blooms exchange giggles amongst the trees.
Ivy's a poet, twisting words so sly,
While ferns tell tales of the clouds rolling by.

Snapdragons snap with a witty jest,
And orchids pose as the elegant best.
"Oh, petal talk!" says the sunflower so bold,
Every charm woven with laughter untold.

Bouncing buds tease the shy moss on the stone,
While wildflowers hop, never alone.
In the garden's embrace, joy we can see,
A comedy found in this floral spree!

The Secret Life of Flora

In a garden where daisies dance,
The tulips plot, they love to prance.
Petunias gossip, oh what a sight,
While cacti chuckle, 'We're just too tight.'

The roses wear hats made of green,
Trying to keep up with the scene.
Lilies complain, 'It's such a chore!'
While violets laugh, 'We want more!'

Tapestry of Tangled Vines

Wisteria weaves tales that perplex,
While ivy ties knots like a fox with specs.
Touch-me-nots giggle, 'Oh, what a mess!'
As the vines hold secrets, in nature's dress.

Grapevines twist in their grand ballet,
While morning glories bloom and sway.
Cucumbers whisper with half-hearted grace,
In this quarrelsome yet lovely place.

Chronicles of the Blooming Heart

Sunflowers reach for the sky, oh dear,
While dandelions scatter without any fear.
A daisy sneezes, causing a fuss,
And bees buzz by, 'We do it for us!'

Hibiscus winks with colorful charm,
Sharing secrets, buzzing like a swarm.
Each bloom with a story, a giggle, a joke,
Life in the garden, a spirited folk.

The Enchanted Orchard

In orchards where apples hang with pride,
The plums roll around, they can't hide.
Cherries giggle, 'What a sweet mess!'
As the oranges plot, 'We'll impress!'

Peaches take selfies, looking quite cute,
While lemons squeeze in, feeling acute.
A pear whispers, 'Let's have a ball,'
In this orchard of laughter, we're having a ball.

The Quill of the Meadow's Muse

In a meadow where daisies giggle,
The sunbeams dance and wildly wiggle.
A squirrel wrote poems on the trees,
With acorn ink, he scribbled with ease.

Oh, the ants formed a line in rhyme,
Chanting verses, keeping time.
A butterfly critiqued with flair,
"Your metaphors need some fresh air!"

The grasshoppers hopped a jig,
While the bees buzzed and did a swig.
With honeyed words they sang with glee,
In this vibrant, silly spree.

When night fell, the fireflies glowed,
As the moonbeam poet, dreams bestowed.
They told tales of a world quite absurd,
Where each leaf spoke, and laughter stirred.

Whispers of the Wandering Winds

The wind brought news of silly things,
Like frogs in boots that dance and sing.
A breeze chuckled, "What a sight!"
As socks flew off in pure delight.

A whisper swirled through trees so grand,
"I've lost my hat, can you lend a hand?"
The leaves would giggle, shaking their tips,
As feathers paraded on breezy trips.

The clouds joined in with fluffy cheers,
Spinning tales and silly queers.
A gust exclaimed, "What's next for me?"
"A dance with rain, or a trip to the sea?"

So twirls and swirls went all around,
As breezy laughs were lost and found.
In this windy world full of jest,
Each gust spread giggles, doing its best.

Traces of Floral Echoes

A flower once tried to tell a joke,
But the tulips just sat, barely woke.
"I'm blooming funny!" it yelled so loud,
Yet all it got was a silence crowd.

The roses blushed, rolled their eyes,
"We've heard that one, oh how time flies!"
But the daisies laughed and clapped their hands,
Even the weeds joined in their plans.

The violets whispered, "Come on, bloom!"
As petals quivered, filling the room.
A garden party with laughter and cheer,
Where even the thorns giggled, never fear!

Then a sunflower stood, bold and bright,
"Why do bees always take flight?"
Buzzing replied, "Because they're so sweet!"
And the flowers just danced to the silly beat.

The Poetry Within the Leaves

In the forest where the critters dwell,
The leaves burst forth with stories to tell.
A birch wrote lines in chunky script,
While the maple sipped tea and unzipped.

"Why did the tree start telling jokes?"
Asked a squirrel, while gathering hoax.
"Because it wanted to branch out more!"
The laughter erupted, an uproar galore.

The oaks made puns, stoic and grand,
Adding humor to their leafy band.
"My bark is worse than my bite, you see!"
Even the mushrooms giggled with glee.

As twilight fell, the giggles grew,
The crickets strummed, planting a clue.
In this leafy world of jokes and plays,
Nature giggled the night away.

The Memory of Swaying Stems

In the garden, a chuckle steals,
A tomato in shorts, how it feels!
The flowers gossip about the bees,
While figs dance on a summer breeze.

Lonely daffodils think they're grand,
Judging the weeds that take a stand.
They swap tales of the sun's warm glow,
As a cabbaged heart steals the show.

A gnome giggles, his hat askew,
He's been planning a grand debut.
With a wink, he tosses some shade,
On the neighbors who care about their grade.

The daisies wink with a giddy cheer,
While marigolds whisper, "Not here, not here!"
In this colorful chaos, we all play,
In the garden of life, come sway away!

Palette of Earthly Whispers

Crayons of green and yellow hues,
Brush the soil with morning dews.
A petunia prances, too loud, too bright,
While roses blush, trying to hide from the light.

Lilies argue over who's more chic,
While buttercups giggle, speaking in Greek.
"Oh darling, your petals clash with this breeze,"
They snicker about her flowery sneeze.

The sun tries to rise, but gets sidetracked,
By the tulips' tales that are never quite packed.
A squirrel interrupts, with a nut in tow,
Saying, "Life's a canvas, put on a show!"

With colors splattered on this grand ground,
The laughter of blooms is a sweet surround.
As the petals swirl 'round in a dance so bold,
They paint the world with stories untold.

Narrative of the Wildflowers

Who knew the violets could write a book?
Giving the daisies a scandalous look!
Their stories of love tangled and sweet,
While sunflowers giggle, hopping on feet.

A dandelion dreams of the skies,
As bumblebees dodge with a little surprise.
"Catch me if you can!" they buzz with glee,
While the clovers roll, hiding in glee.

The lilacs claim they're the wisest of all,
"Here comes trouble!" they quip, as they fall.
The ferns wave and laugh, their fronds in the air,
Saying, "Let's all get tangled, if we dare!"

In fields of chaos, a tale unfolds,
With wildflowers' stories in colors bold.
And as laughter blooms in every line,
Nature's a poet, sipping on sunshine.

Lyrics from the Leafy Canopy

Beneath the branches, a laughter erupts,
As squirrels find acorns, and giggle in slumps.
Leaves rustle softly, sharing the scene,
As the branches sway with a mischief unseen.

The wind pipes a tune, oh so spry,
While a owl winks, and the sparrows fly by.
"Sing higher!" the maples call to the pines,
As nature composes, with rhythm and rhymes.

The berries chime in with fruity delight,
Each note shimmering under the moonlight.
With melodies sweet and laughter abound,
The leafy chorus wraps 'round the ground.

In the canopy's embrace, the stories twist,
Of forest friends that never seem missed.
With a giggle and cheer, we sway hand in hand,
In the leafy symphony of this wondrous land.

The Symphony of Nature's Brush

Bugs in suits dance to the beat,
While flowers gossip on the street.
Each leaf a note, a jovial cheer,
Nature's band plays loud and clear.

The sun wore shades, a dapper glow,
Twirling clouds in a breezy show.
Trees tap their feet in rhythm fine,
A concert where all creatures dine.

Grasshoppers join with a lilting jump,
To the rhythm of a hefty thump.
The daisies sway, heads held so high,
Underneath a blush of sky.

And when the rain begins to pour,
The puddles laugh, asking for more.
A soggy shoe, a lively joke,
In nature's symphony, all have spoke.

Blooms Beneath the Silent Sky

Daffodils don their sunny hats,
As squirrels plot their acorn chats.
Cupcakes of blossoms, sweet delight,
Underneath the starry night.

Tulips whisper tales of glee,
To wandering bees who drink their tea.
The tulip's hat looks quite absurd,
But it's the buzz that's truly heard.

A daisy grins, oh-so-bright,
While chattering frogs croak with delight.
Beneath the moon's wide, glowing grin,
Nature's humor lies within.

The wind tugs gently at the leaves,
Tickling flowers like playful thieves.
Together they twirl, giggle, and spin,
Underneath the dusk, the laughter begins.

Lyrical Meadows Unfurled

Butterflies wear polka-dots,
Spinning tales in sunny spots.
A bumblebee's buzz is quite the tune,
As flowers dance beneath the moon.

Grass blades chuckle, side by side,
As ants march on, full of pride.
Ladybugs play a game of chase,
In the bright and cheerful space.

The wind tells jokes, soft and sweet,
While daisies sway to the upbeat.
In this meadow, laughter sprawls,
Echoing through the leafy halls.

With petals laughing 'neath the sun,
Every moment's a silly run.
Nature's got jokes, you see, my friend,
In lyrical fields that never end.

Echoes in the Wind's Embrace

The breeze giggles as it glides,
Over hills where sparrows bide.
Whispers fly as butterflies soar,
Each rustle's got a tale in store.

A clumsy deer trips by a stream,
Splashing water, what a dream!
Laughter ripples through the air,
Nature's joy is everywhere.

Clouds don hats, fluffy and sleek,
Tickling the mountains on their peak.
The cacti smile, their needles fine,
With cactus jokes, they're quite a line.

The wind's voice, a cheeky tease,
Unwraps laughter from the trees.
With every rustle, cheer we chase,
In echoes found in nature's grace.

Scribe of the Floral Canvas

In a garden of giggles, I scribble with glee,
A daisy told a joke, oh, how funny to see!
Sunflowers dance, twirling their golden hair,
While roses roll their eyes, pretending not to care.

Ladybugs laugh, they're in on the jest,
While ants hold a meeting, they think they're the best.
Butterflies chuckle, wriggling in flight,
Colors swishing like laughs, what a vibrant sight!

Threads of Color

In hues of bright laughter, I weave with delight,
A swirl of the silly, oh what a sight!
Pink threads tickle daisies, yellow ones jest,
Green threads giggle softly, never taking a rest.

The fabric of fun, I stitch and I sew,
Whispers of chuckles in every bright flow.
Blue retracts to tease, while orange plays coy,
The canvas of colors, a tapestry of joy!

Threads of Verse

With threads spun from laughter, I craft every line,
Each rhyme a fine pun, isn't this divine?
A daffodil whispers a joke to a bee,
While violets snicker at the old maple tree.

Each verse is a dance, a giggle untold,
The stanzas keep bouncing, bold and uncontrolled.
Laughter in meters, oh what a sound!
In the garden of words, fun is all around!

The Poetry of Seasons Changing

Spring's laughter bursts forth, a loud raucous cheer,
While winter grumbles softly, still clinging here.
Summer tosses pies, oh what a grand fling,
And autumn snickers, "Look how the leaves cling!"

Each season tells jokes in its own funny way,
With snowflakes like giggles, brightening the gray.
The year spins around, in quips and in jests,
Nature's own humor, it truly invests!

Dances of Petal Poetry

Daffodils twirl, in whims of delight,
While tulips do tango under the moonlight.
Chanting their verses in floral ballet,
A lively performance, come join in the play!

The wind plays a tune, as blossoms all sway,
Petal-full giggles chase worries away.
In this joyous frolic, no frowns can be found,
Just dances of laughter, enchanting and sound!

Unfolding Stories of Nature's Heart

In the garden, plants conspire,
Telling tales of wild desire.
Bees are gossiping, take a guess,
Who knew flowers could cause such a mess?

Sunflowers wear their crowns with pride,
While daisies peek from side to side.
Each bloom a character so bold,
Whispering secrets never told.

Lettuce laughs when the wind's a tease,
Carrots giggle down on their knees.
Nature's heart, a comic stage,
Where every sprout can earn a wage.

Chasing clouds, the tulips dance,
In flamboyant hues, they take their chance.
With laughter echoing through the glade,
They form a circus, nature's parade.

Brushes with Fragrant Wishes

Spray that perfume, oh what a whiff!
Roses giggle, scent's their gift.
Lavender tries to take the lead,
While daisies scheme, 'let's plant a seed!'

Fragrant wishes fill the air,
Scented notes without a care.
Bee and bloom make quite the team,
Painting dreams, or so it seems.

Forget-me-nots whisper, 'Remember me!'
While violets blush, oh how funny to be!
A bouquet mishmash in full display,
Every whiff leads us astray.

Jasmine jewels in the light,
Promising laughter, oh what a sight!
In the garden of whimsical cheer,
Each flower winks, signaling here!

The Haiku of a Blooming Heart

A bud opens wide,
Laughter dances in the breeze,
Nature's heart on cue.

Bees buzzing around,
Practicing sweet melodies,
An orchestra of light.

Petals roll and tumble,
Like socks thrown out in a fit,
Nature's playful prank.

In this garden scene,
Joy blooms from every corner,
Life's a funny dream.

The Aroma of Forgotten Seasons

Spring's caught in a trap,
With autumn's cloak wrapped snug tight.
Scented memories hum,
Whispers of time take flight.

Winter's frost still lingers,
While summer tries to flaunt,
A fragrant tug-of-war,
As flowers scheme and taunt.

Forgotten lavender,
Wonders if she's still in style,
While marigolds conspire,
To outshine each blooming smile.

Seasons trade their jokes,
In the fragrance of old days,
Nature's spiraled laugh,
In a breezy, witty haze.

Nature's Secret Manuscript

In the garden, secrets dwell,
Bugs writing stories, oh so swell.
Bees type buzz, ants spell out,
Nature's laughter, no doubt about.

Flowers gossip, petals shake,
They giggle softly, for goodness' sake.
A squirrel jots down a daring feat,
Under a tree, where laughter's sweet.

Dewdrops glisten, typing at dawn,
Each droplet a verse, a new day drawn.
With a wink, the sun joins in,
Making mischief, where tales begin.

Nature's ink spills, colors swirl,
In this world of whimsy, watch it unfurl.
Each leaf a page, each breeze a laugh,
Writing the script of this quirky path.

Harmonies Among Blooming Fables

In the meadow, stories play,
Flowers croon in a cheery sway.
Butterflies dance in a colorful jig,
While frogs sing a tune, oh so big.

Bees hum sweet, in harmony tight,
Collecting nectar, all day and night.
The daisies chime in, their heads so bold,
With tales of sun and the warmth they hold.

Count the petals, one, two, three,
A debate on who's prettiest, oh dear me!
Laughter echoes, the breeze agrees,
Nature's choir brings the perfect tease.

Each bud's a verse, each bloom a line,
Fables spoken, like moonlit wine.
In this riot of color, oh what fun,
The garden's a novel, never quite done.

Strokes of Green and Gold

On a canvas where critters play,
The brush of nature whirls and sways.
With every stroke, a giggle's found,
In hues of joy, laughter's profound.

Grass tickles toes, and ferns tell tales,
Chasing shadows, where whimsy prevails.
Sunlight's a painter, daubing with cheer,
Crafting delight, year after year.

Golden leaves make a crunchy sound,
As squirrels play tag, round and round.
The canvas shifts, a masterpiece grows,
In the heart of chaos, fun overflows.

Nature's picnic, spread far and wide,
Where laughter and color run side by side.
Brushing life with joy so bold,
In strokes of green, and dashes of gold.

Scented Whispers of the Soul

In the breeze, whispers unfold,
Fragrant secrets, stories told.
Roses giggle, with petals so bright,
Spreading joy from morning till night.

Lavender winks with a calming sigh,
While daisies tease, oh me, oh my!
With scents that dance, and tickle the nose,
They forge a bond, where laughter flows.

Every bloom holds a cheeky grin,
In nature's laugh, we feel the win.
A whiff of joy in the air so clear,
Bringing smiles from ear to ear.

Underneath the stars, flowers sleep,
Dreaming of laughter, secrets they keep.
Scented tales in the cool night dew,
Whispers of joy, written just for you.

Ink and Leaf: A Delicate Tale

In a garden where words take flight,
A quill danced under moonlight.
Ink splattered on a leaf's bright face,
It giggled, oh what a silly place!

A snail claimed it was a writer's error,
As teardrops of dew became a bearer.
The daisies debated their roles as actors,
While the worms spun tales of disaster.

A grape told jokes of wine and cheer,
As bugs laughed loudly, drawing near.
The ink kept spilling, oh what a sight,
A party of thoughts till morning light!

So if you're wandering under the sun,
Remember, it's all just a funny run.
Nature's comedy, what a delight,
Where leaves and ink take flight tonight!

The Ode of Blooming Truths

In the garden of whispers, truth takes a stroll,
A daffodil giggles, playing the role.
It swears the sun wore a silly hat,
While bees buzz loudly, 'Do you hear that?'

A rose declares it's the star of the show,
'I'm fragrant, but look! The daisies glow!'
The tulips shout, 'You're so full of pride,'
While the violets shyly stand side by side.

They plot over tea, the secrets of bloom,
Trading silly stories that fill up the room.
Each petal a page from a funny old book,
Even the fence has a comical look!

So listen closely, next time you roam,
You might hear the garden's joke-laden poem.
Where joy is sprouting with glee and worth,
And laughter's the seed of sweet, silly birth!

Cadence in Color

In the patch where colors collide,
A green leaf tried a dance with pride.
The marigolds laughed, 'What a weird show!'
They twirled in sunshine, putting on a glow.

A blue butterfly sipped on the air,
And whispered secrets without a care.
'Life's a canvas, paint with flair,'
It teased the roses, caught in a snare!

Chasing hues, the petals took flight,
Each one declaring they were just right.
They pranced and pouted, wearing their best,
As colors combined for a silly, wild fest.

So join in the rhythm, it's time to play,
In this wild garden where colors sway.
With laughter and cheer, and a splash of request,
The canvas of life is a marvelous jest!

Tales from the Garden's Whisper

In a garden where chatter is quite the scene,
A carrot crooned songs, oh so green!
'I'm rootin' for laughter, not just for stew,'
It winked at the peas, who giggled too.

The spinach told tales of strength and might,
'I'm powerful, yet soft, in the moonlight.'
The tomatoes chimed in, 'We've stories galore,
Packed with humor, wait, there's more!'

Sunflowers turned, with their heads held high,
'We're mighty tall, oh, don't be shy!'
They towered over, 'Look, we've got shade!'
Mimicking shadows, how comical they've made!

So stroll through the rows and lend them your ear,
These tales of the garden, although quite queer.
Each whisper and chuckle, a flavorful spin,
Where every leaf's laughter is bound to begin!

Musings Beneath the Cherry Tree

Under the boughs, a squirrel prances,
Chasing dreams, and maybe glances.
Dogs look up, they laugh and play,
While cats wear crowns of flowers, hooray!

Beneath the blooms, gossip flows,
About the bees and their fashion shows.
A butterfly flirts, taking a spin,
While ants march by, proud of their kin.

Rumor has it, the wind's in on the joke,
Whispering secrets, chuckles provoke.
Cherry lemonade spills on the ground,
Making a splash, with a giggle sound.

So let's all dance, beneath this tree,
In a waltz with nature, wild and free.
Laughter echoes, joyful and bright,
As we celebrate this whimsical sight.

Chronicles of the Rooted Heart

In gardens green, the worms do waltz,
With a rhythm that's sure to cause some faults.
A bird drops a tune, oh so sweet,
While the flowers tap dance on their feet.

The grass has jokes that go right over heads,
While daisies giggle, under their spreads.
With every tickle of sun and breeze,
Nature's laugh is enough to tease!

Roots gossip low, with secrets to share,
As the daisies play truth or dare.
Each stem has a tale, so fun and sly,
A world of whimsy beneath the sky.

So pull up a chair, get cozy and hear,
The chronicles penned, full of cheer.
With every chuckle, life's a reveal,
In this garden of laughter, it's all very real!

The Story Behind the Bloom

Amidst the petals, tales unfold,
Of flowers dishing dirt, oh so bold.
The rose met the bee, with a wink and a buzz,
Spilling secrets, just because!

Tulips raise eyebrows at the daffodils,
"Why wear a crown, when you can have frills?"
A sunflower spins, twisting with flair,
In the garden, style is quite rare!

Every bud's a character, quirky and grand,
Sharing secrets only they understand.
With every flick of the breeze, here's the plot,
Nature's tale is funny, believe it or not!

So let's gather round, in colors so bright,
For stories that bloom in the warm sunlight.
With laughter and smiles, we're never alone,
In nature's own world, we've all found a home!

Illustrations of Nature's Canvas

In the meadow, art comes alive,
With daisies who dabble, like bees they thrive.
Buttercups color, with glee on display,
While dandelions wish, they could have their say.

A rogue squirrel sketches, with acorn and leaf,
Adding mischief, beyond belief!
The clouds giggle, with a fluffy embrace,
As nature's brushes paint every place.

The twisting vines waltz, hand in hand,
Creating masterworks, oh so grand!
Each petal a stroke, every leaf a line,
In this funny gallery, we've all learned to shine.

So join the canvas, let laughter be heard,
Where even the silence can tickle a word.
With nature's art show, we dance and we play,
Illustrating joy, in our own special way!

Stanzas of the Morning Dew

The grass is a theater, a stage of bright hue,
Where ants do ballet, their dance quite askew.
A ladybug giggles, so round and so proud,
As morning unfolds like a whimsical shroud.

Frogs croak in chorus, a wacky old choir,
As snails race each other, their shells full of fire.
Dewdrops are jewels; the sun winks, so sly,
While butterflies plot their next silly high fly.

Canopy of Colorful Confessions

A tree with a hat made of leaves that are bright,
Holds secrets of squirrels who party all night.
They sip on the nectar from flowers in bloom,
And trade tales of mischief while dodging the gloom.

The wind is a gossip, it whispers and twirls,
Tickling the blossoms, oh how the fun swirls!
Rooted in laughter, the ground shakes with cheer,
As petals eavesdrop, pretending to hear.

Petal-Skinned Stories

In the garden of chatter, strange stories unfold,
A gnome paints with colors, so vivid, so bold.
He tells of a snail who dreamed of a race,
And outran the shadows, a bright smile on face.

With flowers as capes, they soar through the air,
While bees hold awards for best dance and best flair.
The daisies chuckle, as petals confide,
In tales of wild fetches, with ants as the guide.

Gentle Waves of Garden Reverie

The daisies are surfers on ripples of green,
Riding the breezes, their joy is serene.
A lilac once whispered her secrets to bees,
Who buzzed back in laughter, 'We're busy, oh please!'

A worm with a top hat conducts an old band,
While blossoms take flight, like marbles unplanned.
Between twirls and spins, the garden does sway,
In laughter, the blooms all forget about day.

Inspirations Woven in Green

In the garden, frogs debunk,
Wearing hats made of old junk.
They chat over tea, oh so spry,
While butterflies giggle as they fly.

Gnomes dance on the lawn, what a sight,
Twisting their beards left and right.
With a wink and a silly twerk,
They prove mischief can be hard work.

Squirrels gather nuts for a feast,
Telling tales about the wild beast.
One claims it wore a crown of leaves,
And the world giggles, as it believes.

Laughter blooms among the weeds,
As nature feeds the heart's needs.
In this whimsical, green parade,
All serious thoughts begin to fade.

Whimsy of the Wandering Breeze

The breeze tiptoes, a playful tease,
Whispering secrets to the trees.
It swirls around with laughter bright,
Playing tag with the day and night.

Chasing dandelions here and there,
It holds a curious, tangled hair.
Flowers giggle, swaying along,
As wind drafts a silly, soft song.

A leaf competes in a wild race,
Until it trips and lands with grace.
The breeze just winks and gives a shove,
Creating chaos, laughter, and love.

Moths in the moonlight join the dance,
While stars twinkle, don their prance.
Each gust carries dreams unspun,
As daylight fades, and night has begun.

Pagodas of Fragrant Petals

In pagodas made of fragrant blooms,
Bees hum tunes in sunny rooms.
Every flower wears a hat,
A bee's delight in a floral chat.

Raccoons play peek-a-boo with bees,
While squirrels raid their pantry with ease.
Who knew flowers held such fun?
Each petal's a party, second to none!

A daisy decides to stand up tall,
And jokes that it's hosting a grand ball.
With colors swirling, a vibrant show,
Even the garden gnome shimmies low.

The breeze joins in this fragrant fest,
As chubby bumblebees do their best.
In this world where silliness reigns,
Each petal's laughter forever remains.

The Sweet Surrender of the Season

When summer bids a cheeky goodbye,
Leaves start twirling, oh my, oh my!
Each fruit hangs low, in a lazy recline,
As the sun sets, sipping on wine.

Autumn arrives with a wink and a grin,
Pinching cheeks, inviting all in.
Pumpkins giggle, all lined in rows,
Joking 'bout ghosts in pointy toes.

They tell tales of quirky runs,
How sweets appeared, and laughter spun.
As sweaters snug in warmth's embrace,
Winter chuckles, "I'll pick up the pace!"

Beneath thick blankets, we cozy in tight,
With cocoa dreams and snowflake delight.
Each season weaves whimsical lore,
As nature wraps us in fun evermore.

Petal-Crafted Tales

Once a flower thought it could sing,
But it didn't have the right kind of zing.
The bees all laughed, buzzing with glee,
"Stick to pollen, dear friend, just be free!"

A daisy dreamed of wearing a crown,
But next to a rose, it just had a frown.
"You wear it well, with thorns and flair,
I'll stick to my field, I won't compare!"

The tulips conspired to throw a grand ball,
But they tripped on their stems and fell with a sprawl.
The daisies rolled over, they couldn't help but grin,
"Next time, just dance, don't run on your skin!"

In a garden full of giggles and cheer,
Laughter grows louder, it's crystal clear.
Each tale that blooms brings a chuckle or two,
In this world of whimsy, just enjoy the view!

Scribbles Beneath the Arbor

Under an oak, a squirrel named Clyde,
Wrote poetry with acorns, filled with pride.
Each rhyme was nuts, they rolled off the page,
Nature's comedian, the forest's best sage!

A ladybug critiqued, with glasses on tight,
"Your verses are charming, but need more flight!"
Clyde just chuckled, and twirled in a spin,
"Next time I'll write with a feathered grin!"

The wind played tricks, rustling leaves loud,
While a lazy caterpillar formed a small crowd.
"Can I read, oh wise one?" it asked with a yawn,
"Only if you promise not to drool on my dawn!"

They scribbled until dusk bathed them in gold,
A story of laughter, just waiting to unfold.
Beneath the oak's branches, nonsense did thrive,
With giggles and wiggles, they felt so alive!

Garden of Fleeting Echoes

In a garden where shadows play peek-a-boo,
A sunflower quipped, "I don't know about you!"
"But I swear I just saw a gnome wink at me,
Or was it just pollen? Oh, wait, it's always free!"

A rose threw a shade and said with a smirk,
"Let's throw a party, let's all go berserk!"
But thorns got too wild, pricking the fun,
So they danced in their pots, one by one.

The violets cracked jokes about bees' busy buzz,
"What do you call them? Oh, that's just a fuzz!"
Even the daisies joined in with delight,
"And what's a bee's favorite snack? Honey bright!"

While poppies whispered secrets to the ground,
Each echo of laughter created a sound.
In a world of chaos, they bloomed with a cheer,
For every note of joy, they held dear.

The Colorful Alchemy of Time

Time said to flowers, "Let's swap our hues!"
The daisies giggled, "Yeah, we've got the blues!"
So tulips turned yellow, roses went green,
In a garden of laughter, they painted the scene.

The clock ticked backward, a quirky old trick,
While petunias posed for a fabulous flick.
"Oh darling, just smile, time can bend,
But keep your roots firm; we don't want to offend!"

A butterfly fluttered, its wings ever bright,
"You all look ridiculous, but what a delight!"
The garden erupted in whimsical cheer,
As colors mingled and rode on a sphere.

"Let's dance till the dusk, our colors collide!"
They hopped to the rhythm, both silly and wide.
In a world where time laughs, and hues intertwine,
Every bloom has its moment, and oh, how they shine!

Fables Beneath the Blossoms

Once a bee wore a tiny hat,
Buzzing proudly, thinking he's quite the brat.
He bumped a bloom, oh what a sight,
Fell into nectar, then took flight!

A snail claimed he could run so fast,
Took off slowly, but fell on grass.
The flowers giggled, what a show,
As the wise old owl muttered, "Oh no!"

The ladybug danced a jig of grace,
Tripped on a leaf, landed on her face.
"Oops!" she laughed, with wings askew,
In this garden, who knew chaos could be so cute?

A wily worm thought he'd play smart,
Try to impress a sweet tomato heart.
He curled up tight, then slipped away,
That veggie just shrugged, said, "Not today!"

The Dance of Dappled Dreams

In the sunlit glade, the frogs did spring,
Each hoping to be crowned the frog king.
They leaped and croaked with all their might,
But all they won was a bug's delight!

A squirrel twirled with a nut galore,
But lost his grip and went for a roll.
He landed soft on a patch of moss,
Laughing, he thought, "What a graceful toss!"

A hedgehog joined, thinking it grand,
To show off his moves, the best in the land.
He spun and twisted, felt like a star,
But poked a friend, and they called it bizarre!

The dance by dusk faded with ease,
When a whiskered cat stretched beneath the trees.
"Join us!" they cheered, but he just clacked,
"I prefer my naps, keep your dance intact!"

Verses Carved in Bark

In the woods, a tree had a story to tell,
Carved by lovers who thought it was swell.
"I love you more than sap and bark!"
A squirrel rolled his eyes, giving a snark.

A woodpecker knocked to join the mix,
"Hey, what's this love? Can I get my fix?"
The tree just chuckled, "You're more than a quack,
But I'm busy holding hearts on my back!"

A rabbit hopped by, curious and bright,
"If love is so great, why take a bite?"
The woodpecker paused, then gave a grin,
"Let's nibble and love, we all can win!"

As night fell soft, stars twinkled high,
The tree sighed gently, watching the sky.
"In each groove and whack, there's laughter and cheer,
Just don't forget, keep the stories near!"

Meadow's Arcadian Ballad

In a meadow bright where the daisies sway,
A cow joined a band that played all day.
With a moo and a twirl, she stole the scene,
"Best udder dancer this side of green!"

A rabbit hopped in, with rhythm and beat,
With paws in the air, he thought it was neat.
The cow giggled sweetly, a gig of delight,
As the band played on under the moonlight.

The sun set low, casting shadows wide,
A fox in a tuxedo appeared with pride.
He twirled a partner that wasn't quite there,
What a sight! A fox dancing through thin air!

With laughter that echoed beneath the stars,
They danced through the night; oh, such silly bars.
The critters all joined—what a magical call,
In the meadow's embrace, there was fun for all!

The Lyrics of Lush Existence

In gardens where the daisies dance,
The bumblebees forget their chance.
They buzz and giggle all around,
While clumsy flies just bump and bound.

The roses wear their thorns with pride,
While tulips try to act their size.
A sunbeam tickles every leaf,
And laughter's found in every chief.

A squirrel steals all the walnuts back,
While grasshoppers provide the snack.
With each sprout, a joke is told,
In whispers only blooms behold.

So take a stroll through this delight,
Where every plant can crack a bite.
For nature here, with humor's grace,
Leaves giggles in a leafy space.

Silhouettes of Verdant Wishes

In shadows deep where wishes grow,
The playful winds begin to blow.
They tease the trees with secrets bold,
While whispering tales of green and gold.

The lilies laugh, they spin and sway,
Dreaming of becoming frogs someday.
Their petals shyly nod and wink,
While dragonflies just stop to think.

Each fern is bent on making fun,
To outsmart every lazy sun.
They wiggle, giggle, twist and twirl,
In a bright, green-tinted whirl.

So come and hear the chuckles near,
In every leaf, a joke, a cheer.
For in the greenery, glee will sprout,
And nature's laughter is about.

The Colorful Serenade of Growth

A garden sings in hues so bright,
With flowers winking in delight.
The daisies strut in twirling dress,
While sunflowers just can't help but bless.

The marigolds throw a fiesta grand,
While violets form a lively band.
Each bloom a note, each stem a tale,
As bees hum softly, like a gale.

The zinnias gossip, oh so loud,
They're the stars of the floral crowd.
A rainbow's laugh spills on the ground,
While petals tremble, joy unbound.

So join the chorus, give a cheer,
For growth is funny when we're near.
In colors bright, let laughter reign,
In nature's song, all joy remain.

Echoes of Nature's Heartbeat

Beneath the trees where shadows play,
A chorus of chirps greets the day.
The crickets chirp their evening tune,
While owls wink under the silver moon.

The frogs croak jokes from muddy beds,
While snails slide in their slimy threads.
The chatter in the underbrush,
Makes even brambles start to blush.

With every rustle, giggles rise,
As butterflies wear their best disguise.
In fields where daisies have their say,
Nature's humor comes out to play.

So listen close and you might hear,
The echoing laughter drawing near.
For in the wild where life's a beat,
Fun blooms beneath the dancer's feet.

Inked Blooms Beneath the Moon

Under the moon, flowers dance bright,
Telling secrets in the cool night.
A daisy whispers, brimming with sass,
"Why don't roses ever mow their grass?"

Jokes flying like petals on wind,
A tulip chuckles, it's quite the trend.
"Why did the lily bring a chair?"
"To relax, of course! Who else would care?"

Inky drops on their fancy attire,
They giggle and twirl, never to tire.
Butterflies swoosh in with a grin,
"Who knew a garden could be such a win?"

With laughter echoing 'neath silver beams,
These floral jesters live out their dreams.
Whimsy trailing in each rustling leaf,
They bloom in joy, sans worry or grief.

Fragrance of Stanzas

A daffodil crafted rhymes so sweet,
While daisies danced to the beat of their feet.
"What smells worse than the gym on a dash?"
"A compost heap that turned to a mash!"

Cacti chimed in, spiky and bold,
"Our lines are sharp, but the truth is told!"
They laughed at the ferns, with curls so tight,
"We grow without worry, that's our delight!"

With scent of the tape, the verses took flight,
As bees joined the fun, buzzing with might.
"What did the lavender say to the thyme?"
"We'd make a great pair, just give it some time!"

In a cloud of aroma, the poems arose,
Each line a petal, a fragrant prose.
They savored the joy, sipping dew with glee,
In the garden of words, forever carefree.

Elegies for the Garden's Heart

In memory of blooms that wilted away,
The roses held gatherings, what a display!
"Why did the fern join the sad song?"
"It thought it could finally belong!"

The daisies reminisced, laughing with tears,
"Remember that time we chased away fears?"
With petals like banners, they waved at the sky,
"Don't worry, dear friends, we'll give this a try!"

Mourning the past, but laughing quite loud,
"What's with the gloom?" asked a particularly proud.
"Why mourn for the blooms that didn't last long?"
"Let's celebrate life with a giggle and song!"

Each with a story, they sowed seeds anew,
In this garden of laughter, banded and true.
Elegies spoken with joy in their heart,
From ashes to laughter, a blossoming art.

Silhouettes of Quiet Beauty

In the dusk light, shadows pranced and played,
With laughter and giggles, a silly charade.
The violets whispered, "Did you see that dance?"
"That bug just slipped! I can't take a chance!"

Dandelions, bold, blew wishes so wild,
"Sometimes, being a weed is quite the styled!"
"What's funnier than a squirrel in a hat?"
"A sunflower giggling at a sleepy cat!"

Silhouettes swaying, a calming breeze flows,
In their quiet beauty, everyone knows,
"Why do we love this garden of fun?"
"Because here, together, we all are one!"

So they gather close, beneath the soft glow,
Where vines twist and twine in an evening's flow.
Memories etched in their leafy embrace,
With laughter and love, they all found their place.

Whispers of Blossom

In a garden filled with chatter,
Tulips giggle, making me flatter.
Daisies dance with clumsy grace,
While sunflowers plot in a leafy race.

A rose leans in with a juicy tale,
Of a bee who tried but would not prevail.
Laughter echoes through the green,
As the petals tease in a floral scene.

The violets whisper secrets of woe,
How daisies dared to steal their show.
But in the end, they all agree,
That bloomers will always be frolicsome and free.

So here we sit with our funny blooms,
Giggling softly in nature's rooms.
Life's a jest among green and bright,
In the garden where laughter takes flight.

Verses of the Florals

Oh, the pansies wear their mismatched hues,
A fashion show for critters to peruse.
With every bloom, a new outfit to flaunt,
While bees buzz by, giving flowers a taunt.

The irises gossip, their heads held high,
About the roses who are far too shy.
With petals like velvet, they make quite a fuss,
Claiming fragrance gives them a glorious plus.

When the daisies tell a corny joke,
Even cacti chuckle; they can't help but poke.
In this floral assembly, oh what a sight,
As laughter sways under the warm sunlight.

So gather 'round, you blooms of every shade,
Let's celebrate the fun that we've made.
Each verse a chuckle, a giggle, a cheer,
In glorious gardens, we hold dear.

The Language of Bloom

Listen close, the flowers do speak,
With jokes and jests, not for the meek.
A tulip's wink can halt your stride,
While a petunia sidles up with pride.

Every blossom has its own flair,
With tales of breeze and sun in the air.
A marigold chuckles, a cunning sly,
While daisies laugh beneath the sky.

The lilacs sway, stirring up the fun,
Mixing their scents, oh what a run!
With petals as pages, they scribble and play,
Crafting a script of a sunshiny day.

So dance with me in this floral parade,
Where every bloom has a joke to upgrade.
In this garden of giggles, we'll write a new tune,
As laughter floats high like a bright afternoon.

Swaying with the Petal-drift

Winds carry tales from the flora up high,
While daisies spin dreams in a blushing sky.
The wind whispers secrets, oh what a show,
As lilacs trip gracefully, stealing the flow.

A dandelion's wish goes tumbling about,
While petunias smile, joining the shout.
The fuchsia plays tricks, oh what a tease,
Making the busy bees giggle with ease.

In this cheerful grove where colors collide,
Every bloom is a jest; there's nowhere to hide.
They blossom and bend, a comical twist,
Inventing the humor that nature insists.

So sway with me in this garden of cheer,
Where laughter and love fill the atmosphere.
With petals aglow and spirits so bright,
We dance through the day, in the soft twilight.

www.ingramcontent.com/pod-product-compliance
Lightning Source LLC
Chambersburg PA
CBHW071835160426
43209CB00003B/307